The Military History of World War II: Volume 4

THE NAVAL WAR
IN THE WEST
The Raiders

by Trevor Nevitt Dupuy
COL., U.S. ARMY, RET.

FRANKLIN WATTS, INC.
575 Lexington Avenue • New York 22

To George

Library of Congress Catalog Card Number: 63-9796
Copyright © 1963 by Franklin Watts, Inc.
Printed in the United States of America

3   4   5   6   7

Contents

SEA POWER SHAPES THE WAR   1

The Athenia, 1
Britain and Sea Power, 3
Germany's Naval Strategy, 6

THE FIRST THREE MONTHS   10

The Courageous *and the* Royal Oak, 10
Countering the U-Boats and Magnetic Mines, 12
Surface Raiders and the Rawalpindi, 15

THE CRUISE OF THE *Graf Spee*   16

Scourge of the South Atlantic, 18
Harwood's Hunch, 20
The Battle of the River Plate, 20
The End of the Graf Spee, 23

THE WAR GETS HOTTER   25

   The "Phony War," 25
   The Altmark *Affair*, 26
   Eyes on Norway, 27
   Germany Invades Norway, 29
   The "Miracle of Dunkirk," 34

THE DARK DAYS OF 1940   35

   The Shifting Balance of Sea Power, 35
   The French Fleet, 37
   Objective: Britain, 40
   A Success and a Failure, 43

THE NAVAL STRUGGLE FOR THE MEDITERRANEAN   44

   Early Engagements, 44
   The Attack on Taranto, 46
   German Intervention in the Mediterranean, 48
   Battle of Cape Matapan, 49
   Greece and Crete, 51

THE RAIDERS   53

   The Scheer *and the* Jervis Bay, 53
   Hipper, Scharnhorst, *and* Gneisenau, 55
   The Cruise of the Bismarck *and the* Prinz Eugen, 55
   The Battle of Denmark Strait, 59
   The Chase, 60
   The Search, 61

INDEX   66

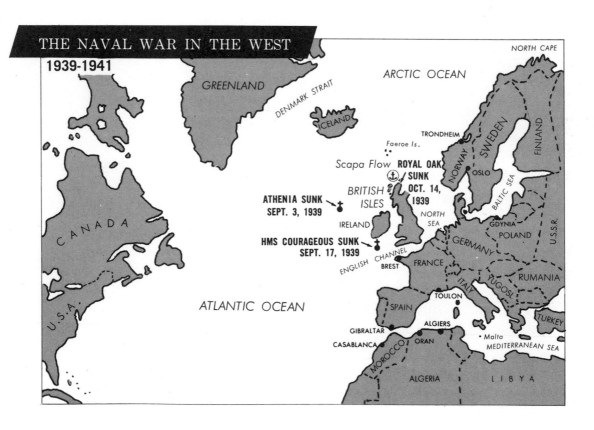

THE NAVAL WAR IN THE WEST

1939-1941

NORTH CAPE

ARCTIC OCEAN

GREENLAND

DENMARK STRAIT

ICELAND

Faeroe Is.

TRONDHEIM

SWEDEN

NORWAY

FINLAND

OSLO

BALTIC SEA

Scapa Flow **ROYAL OAK SUNK OCT. 14, 1939**

BRITISH ISLES

NORTH SEA

GDYNIA

U.S.S.R.

ATHENIA SUNK SEPT. 3, 1939

IRELAND

GERMANY

POLAND

HMS COURAGEOUS SUNK SEPT. 17, 1939

ENGLISH CHANNEL

BREST

FRANCE

RUMANIA

ITALY

YUGOSL

CANADA

TOULON

ATLANTIC OCEAN

SPAIN

TURKEY

GIBRALTAR

ALGIERS

U.S.A.

CASABLANCA

ORAN

Malta

MEDITERRANEAN SEA

MOROCCO

ALGERIA

LIBYA

Sea Power Shapes the War

The Athenia

ON SEPTEMBER 3, 1939, two days after Hitler's treacherous attack on Poland, Great Britain declared war on Germany, and a radio warning went out from London to all the British ships at sea.

The message was received on the British passenger liner *Athenia*, which had left Britain the day before, bound for New York. The *Athenia*, then northwest of Ireland, at once began to sail a zigzag course so that she would not make a good target for German submarines that might be lurking nearby. As night fell, the ship was blacked out, and continued to steam westward on her jerky course in complete darkness.

Nearly 1,500 people, including both passengers and crew, were on board the ship, and they were all excited by the news that war had been declared between Great Britain and Germany. Many of the passengers were American tourists, rushing home to escape the war that had just broken out in Poland.

At 9:00 P.M. there was a terrific explosion; the *Athenia* shuddered and lurched. She had been struck by a torpedo. Radio messages had gone out over the oceans from Berlin as well as from London. German submarine *U-30* had received the message, and was waiting. Even in the gloom of night, the sharp-eyed U-boat captain had seen the darkened *Athenia* as she passed by. Without warning, he had fired his torpedo with deadly accuracy.

One hundred and twelve people lost their lives in the sinking of the *Athenia* — twenty-eight of them American citizens. Most of the world was horrified. People in the United States were angry and indignant. To try to appease American public opinion, Hitler im-

The British fleet at Malta. From 1940-1943 the island of Malta endured thousands of attacks from German planes.

mediately ordered his submarine crews not to attack any more passenger ships. The German radio tried to tell the world that the *Athenia* had not been sunk by a torpedo, but that it had been blown up by a bomb which the British themselves had placed on the ship to make Americans angry at Germany. Few people, however, were fooled by this false propaganda.

Compared to the millions who were to die in this terrible war, only a few lives were lost on the *Athenia*. The importance of the tragic event was in what it symbolized. British merchant shipping was menaced from the very outset of the war by German submarines manned by coldly efficient crews, responsive immediately to the ruthless control of Hitler's Nazi government.

Britain and Sea Power

THE DAY before war was declared, Prime Minister Neville Chamberlain of Great Britain had appointed Winston Churchill to be the First Lord of the Admiralty, which is the same thing as the American Secretary of the Navy. Chamberlain knew that as a young man, twenty-five years earlier, Churchill had been in the same job, and had prepared the British navy to fight in World War I. Every Englishman knew that Churchill understood the Royal Navy better than any other civilian. And British sailors knew that he had the character, strength of will, and wisdom to direct that Navy superbly. The day he was appointed, the Navy sent out a message to all of its ships: "Winston is back." Prime Minister Chamberlain had made many mistakes in the months before World War II. His appointment of Churchill to the Admiralty made up for some of them.

Churchill understood very well how important sea power was to the survival of his country. Great Britain was an island that could produce only half of the food consumed by its 50,000,000 inhabitants. The other half had to be brought in by ships. In addition, if the great British factories were to turn out guns, aircraft, tanks, warships, trucks, and all the other equipment necessary to fight a war, ships would also have to bring iron, lumber, oil, and many other resources, for Great Britain had few raw materials.

Churchill remembered that in World War I the German U-boats had sunk so many British merchant ships that England had come very close to starvation. He realized that submarines were the greatest threat his navy had to face in this new war. He was not much concerned about the German surface warships — there were very few compared to the great numbers of powerful ships of the Royal Navy and the additional strength of the French navy. (See the Table of Comparative Strengths on page 9.) But Churchill was very worried because Britain had so few cruisers and destroyers. These were the only kinds of ships that were fast enough to be used effectively against U-boats.

There were millions upon millions of square miles of ocean surface where British merchant ships were carrying valuable cargo to or from Britain. The German submarines could secretly appear anyplace, sink a British ship, then slink away under the surface of the ocean. The available destroyers and cruisers could protect only a tiny fraction of that vast water surface, and they could never tell where the U-boats would strike next.

Immediately after the *Athenia* was sunk, Churchill ordered the establishment of a convoy system to protect merchant ships. This was an arrangement in which large numbers of merchant ships were collected into a group, or convoy. These vessels then sailed together as a group, protected by an escort of several fast warships, usually cruisers or destroyers. This system had worked in World War I, but the Royal Navy had had many more cruisers and destroyers in that war, and German submarines had been neither so big nor so fast as they were in 1939. At the beginning of World War II England had few escort warships available to protect her convoys; there were so few, in fact, that convoys could be used only in the most dangerous waters of the eastern part of the North Atlantic Ocean, where the sea-lanes came together near Britain.

Although submarines were the greatest danger to British shipping, they were not the only danger. Germany had two big battle cruisers ready for combat, along with three "pocket" battleships and two heavy cruisers, all of them newer, faster, and more powerful than any British heavy cruiser.

To keep these big ships from getting out to raid the sea-lanes, the British had to do two things. First, they had to patrol all of the sea approaches to Germany through the English Channel and the North Sea. Part of this patrol task could be done by long-range aircraft, but many cruisers and destroyers were also needed — particularly for stormy weather when airplanes could not see the surface of the sea. Next, in case one or more of these big German ships broke out, British surface forces — including battleships and aircraft carriers — had to be ready to give chase. But these larger British ships could not venture out to sea without protection against German submarines, and such protection could be given only by cruisers and destroyers.

The British also had to keep constantly in mind the possibility that Premier Benito Mussolini, Fascist dictator of Italy, and Hitler's Axis partner, might bring his country into the war. That would mean the outbreak of a naval war in the Mediterranean Sea.

Through the Mediterranean ran one of the principal sea-lanes over which vital raw materials were brought to England. This lane

5

was also the route by which the British would send troops and military supplies to colonies in the Mediterranean, East Africa, and Asia. And along this same sea-lane would come reinforcements from India, Australia, and New Zealand to help the outnumbered British fight the Germans. So important was this watery line of communications that it was called "Britain's lifeline." The Royal Navy had to keep a strong force in the Mediterranean if England was to continue fighting the war. And this meant fewer cruisers and destroyers to protect the Atlantic convoys.

Another important task of the Royal Navy was to establish a naval blockade that would cut off all of Germany's sea trade. Germany was not as dependent as Britain on overseas commerce. Across those of its frontiers that abutted on friendly and neutral nations, Germany could receive raw materials by railroad. But the German railroads were already busy with their normal traffic, as well as with heavy movements of military supplies and troops. The British knew that it would be very difficult and expensive for the Germans to get goods from overseas in this indirect fashion. In World War I the British naval blockade of Germany had been one of the most important causes of the Allied victory.

Germany's Naval Strategy

THE NAVAL PROBLEMS of Germany were much simpler than those of Great Britain. German sailors realized that they could not hope to fight many surface sea battles against the much larger Royal Navy. And they knew that they could not prevent the British blockade from cutting off all of their overseas commerce through the North Sea and Atlantic Ocean.

So the German navy was left with only two main missions. The first of these was to retain control of the Baltic Sea, and of the short, easily defended sea-lanes from Germany to Norway and Sweden. These lanes were vital to German war production because most of Germany's iron ore came from mines in Sweden and was shipped to Germany either across the Baltic Sea, or through the coastal waters of Norway. Germany's small surface fleet was adequate to control the Baltic against any possible unfriendly combination of Baltic nations. The Germans were certain that British surface ships could not get to the Baltic, because they could not pass through the narrow Scandinavian Straits without being smashed by German air power.

The second German naval mission was the one Churchill feared most: to attack British merchant shipping. The submarine was expected to be the main weapon in these attacks, but surface ships, airplanes, and submarine mines were also expected to play important parts.

Germany had learned many lessons from World War I, when its submarines had come close to defeating Britain. After that war German sailors had studied how to correct the mistakes they had made, and how to use their bigger and better U-boats more effectively if they had to fight again. In addition, they knew that their surface ships could make the British defensive task more difficult by dashing out of the North Sea under cover of bad weather to attack single merchant ships, or convoys protected by small cruisers and destroyers. Such attacks would also force the British to divert some of their scarce warships from antisubmarine warfare to escort duty. The U-boats would be able to sink more British ships while German surface raiders were operating in the North Sea.

7

On top of that, German long-range aerial bombers could attack British ports, sinking ships in harbor and destroying the docks where goods were loaded and unloaded. And finally, the German navy was ready with some newly developed and particularly deadly submarine mines that could be laid off the British coast by destroyers, submarines, and aircraft.

And so, as war became imminent, Grand Admiral Erich Raeder, commanding the German navy, sent out a number of his submarines to wait on the North Atlantic sea-lanes. It was one of these that sank the *Athenia*. At the same time, the pocket battleships *Graf Spee* and *Deutschland* were cruising in the Atlantic, and arrangements had been made to keep them supplied with fuel from secretly dispatched German tankers. The German navy was ready.

German submarine flotilla at Kiel, waiting for orders to prowl the North Atlantic sea-lanes in search of British transport ships.

September, 1939

COMPARATIVE NAVAL STRENGTHS[1]

	Britain	France	Germany[2]	Italy
Battleships and Battle Cruisers[3]	18	11	4	6
"Pocket" Battleships[4]	-	-	3	-
Aircraft Carriers	10	1	1	-
Heavy Cruisers (8″ guns or more)	15	18	4	7
Light Cruisers (6″ guns or less)	62	32	6	15
Destroyers	205	34	25	59
Destroyer Escorts, Torpedo Boats, etc.	73	30	42	69
Motor Torpedo Boats	39	9	17	69
Submarines	70	72	98	115

[1] Includes ships built or nearing completion.

[2] All German vessels were newly built, and with few exceptions were more modern, faster, bigger, and generally more powerful than comparable types of other nations.

[3] Battle cruisers were as big as battleships and carried the same kind of heavy guns (usually 14″ to 16″ in caliber). But they carried less armor protection, and usually fewer heavy guns, so that, being lighter in weight, they could go faster than battleships. Thus they could hit as hard as battleships, but could not take as much punishment; they sacrificed protection for speed.

[4] Under the provisions of the Versailles Treaty after World War I, Germany was forbidden to build ships larger than 10,000 tons. The pocket battleships were really small battle cruisers; they carried 11″ guns, were very fast, but did not have much armor, so that they would not exceed the weight limit. They could beat any cruiser in the world, but could not stand up to a real battleship.

The First Three Months

The Courageous *and the* Royal Oak

IMMEDIATELY war was declared, both the German and British navies went about their tasks in the most efficient and determined manner. Each was able to inflict some unpleasant surprises on the other, but neither was able to gain a decisive advantage.

During the first six weeks of the war, Germany gained two dramatic naval successes. Although the main mission of the German submarines was to attack merchant shipping, they were even more anxious to sink British warships, the larger the better. The most rewarding target a U-boat captain could hope for would be a battleship or an aircraft carrier. But there were very few chances to attack such ships, because they were always so closely defended by smaller, faster warships.

On September 17, 1939, the British aircraft carrier HMS *Courageous*, protected by four destroyers, was cruising off the southwest coast of England. Here many sea-lanes came together, and so the planes of the *Courageous* were out scouting for U-boats and protecting incoming merchant ships. At dusk the great vessel turned into the wind to take her planes back on board. At that very moment she was struck by a torpedo from the German submarine *U-29*. She sank at once. Of the nearly 1,300 men carried by the *Courageous*, more than 500 were lost.

Most of the large British ships were at the Scapa Flow naval anchorage in the Orkney Islands, off the north coast of Scotland. Here there was a wide basin of water, completely surrounded by islands, with only a few narrow, winding channels through which ships could pass. The main passages were covered by steel submarine nets and guarded by patrol vessels. All other entrances were blocked by bar-

British battleship HMS Royal Oak, *sunk at anchorage in Scapa Flow by the German submarine U-47.*

ges or old ships sunk across the narrow channels between the islands. In this protected anchorage the British ships were almost out of reach of the longest-range German bombers. At the same time the fleet was in a position to move out quickly to meet any German surface raider trying to get out of the North Sea.

Shortly after midnight on October 14, Lieutenant Commander Gunther Prien brought the submarine *U-47* just outside the islands surrounding Scapa Flow. Skillfully he piloted his vessel between two blockships that had been sunk to plug one of the minor channels into the anchorage. Navigating the narrow opening, with its rapid, swirling tides, was a great feat of seamanship by Prien. As the darkened U-boat silently and slowly slipped past the island shore, she was so close to land that Prien could see an unsuspecting cyclist pedaling past him on the coastal road.

Once inside the anchorage, the submarine crept silently forward. Then suddenly the Germans saw ahead the great bulk of a British battleship. Submerging slightly, Prien fired four torpedoes. "Then," according to the German report, "came a shattering explosion, and a great pillar of water rose in the darkness." Quickly reloading, the German submarine fired again. This time all four torpedoes hit the battleship. It was HMS *Royal Oak*. She sank almost at once, carrying down 786 officers and men.

Soundlessly the *U-47* slipped back through the same channel by which she had come. Prien had successfully completed one of the great exploits of the war.

Countering the U-Boats and Magnetic Mines

GERMAN submarines sank twelve British merchant ships in the first week of the war, and eleven more in the second week. Then, during the last two weeks of September, when the British convoy system began to operate, they succeeded in sinking only three, making a total of 26 during the month. In October submarines counted 14 victims, but only five in November. By then British shipyards were building ships faster than they were being sunk. Churchill could rightly claim that the convoy system was beating the U-boats.

On the other hand, this same convoy system had greatly slowed down the flow of raw materials and goods to and from England. Even though the ships were loaded and ready to leave port, they had to wait until enough supplies were gathered to make the convoy worth while. And all the ships had to go at the pace of the slowest.

Churchill was alarmed at this slowing down of shipments of needed war materials. He wrote to his staff: "We shall have failed in our task if we merely substitute delays for sinkings." Under his driving leadership the convoy system was speeded up and made more efficient. Also, as soon as guns could be mounted on them, those cargo vessels that could travel fast enough to evade U-boats were allowed to sail through the danger zones alone. The British shipping rate soon rose, while losses to submarines remained low.

Then the Germans introduced a new magnetic mine that would explode if a ship passed nearby, even if it did not touch the mine. This meant that the minesweepers, too, would blow up as they tried to sweep the mines out of the shipping channels. In September and October a few ships had been sunk by these new explosive devices off the English coast. As more and more magnetic mines were laid by German submarines and aircraft, British shipping losses rose sharply. Thirteen British ships and a number of neutral vessels were sunk by magnetic mines in November.

Then a brave crew of British sailors, experts in mine warfare, found a magnetic mine in shallow water. At the risk of being blown

This U-boat surfaced to recharge its batteries and was immediately attacked and sunk by British planes.

to pieces at any minute, they took the mine apart and discovered how it worked.

By the end of November these experts had discovered a way to neutralize the magnetic effect of the mines. This was done by winding an electric cable around the hull of a ship, and then passing a constant electric current through the cable. All British merchant ships and warships were quickly equipped with these "degaussing cables," as they were called, and losses from magnetic mines began to drop sharply.

Surface Raiders and the Rawalpindi

As we have seen, the German pocket battleships *Graf Spee* and *Deutschland* were at sea when the war began. The *Graf Spee* was in the South Atlantic, while the *Deutschland* waited quietly off the east coast of Greenland. Not until late September, when Hitler realized that Britain and France would not make peace after his conquest of Poland, did he permit the two warships to start their attacks.

Close-up of a German U-boat, showing conning tower and periscope.

The *Deutschland* sailed south to the main North Atlantic sea-lanes. In October she sank two British merchant ships, and created an international incident by seizing the neutral American freighter, *City of Flint*. Then, plagued with engine trouble, the *Deutschland* headed back toward Germany in November.

The German naval staff now decided to send out two battle cruisers, the *Scharnhorst* and the *Gneisenau*, to cover the withdrawal of the *Deutschland* and to harass British shipping. Late in December, the two ships slipped past the patrols east of Scotland, but on December 23 they were sighted by the British vessel *Rawalpindi* between Iceland and the group of islands known as the Faeroes. The *Rawalpindi* was an armed merchant cruiser, a hastily converted passenger liner on which four 6-inch guns had been mounted.

As soon as she sighted the two battle cruisers, the *Rawalpindi* sent out a radio warning to all other British ships at sea. Then she bravely turned to meet her two giant antagonists. A few minutes later she was a sinking mass of wreckage. But the British fleet was gathering, and the two German ships decided that they had best return to their base in Germany. The valiant *Rawalpindi* had sacrificed herself to keep the blockade tight.

The Cruise of the *Graf Spee*

Scourge of the South Atlantic

LATE IN SEPTEMBER, 1939, Captain Hans Langsdorf, commanding the German pocket battleship *Graf Spee*, received orders to begin operations against British merchant shipping. Until he received this order, Langsdorf had kept his ship cruising quietly in areas of the

The German pocket battleship Graf Spee *at anchor off Uruguay. In 1939, in the space of two months, this raider captured and sank nine British ships.*

South Atlantic Ocean far away from the regular sea-lanes. Now he moved into the main shipping track between Pernambuco, Brazil, and Cape Town, South Africa.

Soon he seized a victim. He took off the British crew, then sank the vessel. British warships and aircraft tried to find Langsdorf, but immediately after the sinking he turned away from the sea-lane. A few days later, several hundred miles away, he repeated the bold capture and sinking. Then again he disappeared from the sea-lanes.

For more than two months Langsdorf continued to appear and disappear. During that time he captured and sank nine British ships. He ranged all over the South Atlantic, and even ventured into the

17

Indian Ocean. The importance of what the *Graf Spee* was doing is shown by the number of Allied ships that were gathered to chase her: two British aircraft carriers, one British battle cruiser, four British heavy cruisers, two French heavy cruisers, two British light cruisers, and at least ten Allied destroyers.

Late in November Captain Langsdorf made a secret rendezvous at sea with the German fuel and supply ship *Altmark*. The *Graf Spee* filled her fuel tanks with oil, took on supplies, and transferred more than 300 British prisoners to the *Altmark*. The pocket battleship then returned to her prowling search for victims. She found one in the middle of the South Atlantic on December 2, and another on December 3. Four days later, and more than a thousand miles to the west, she sank another British ship.

Harwood's Hunch

DURING the last days of November, a British force of two heavy cruisers and two light cruisers was patrolling off the east coast of South America, hoping to catch the *Graf Spee*. Commanding this squadron was Commodore Henry Harwood.

Harwood had been studying his ocean charts and marking the positions of each victim of the *Graf Spee*. He thought he detected a pattern in the German operations. Then, when he received radio reports of the sinkings on December 2, 3, and 7, he was convinced that the pocket battleship was heading toward the crowded shipping lanes leading to Buenos Aires and Montevideo, off the mouth of the River Plate, in South America.

Harwood immediately radioed his scattered vessels to gather off the River Plate by December 12. He expected that Langsdorf and the *Graf Spee* would arrive in that area on December 13. Unfortun-

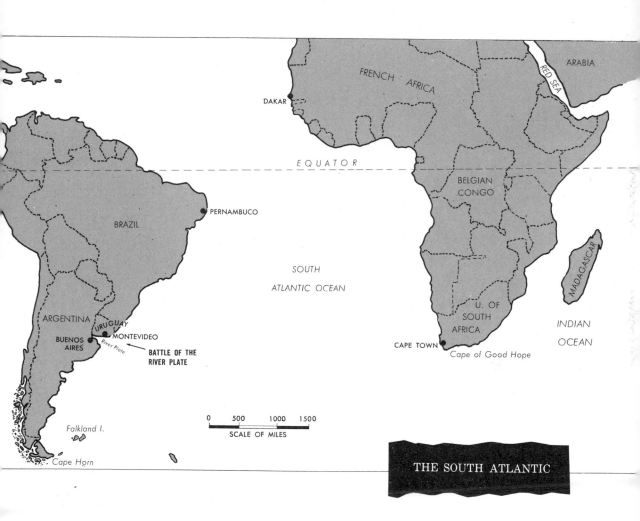

ARABIA

RED SEA

FRENCH AFRICA

DAKAR

EQUATOR

BELGIAN
CONGO

PERNAMBUCO

BRAZIL

MADAGASCAR

SOUTH

ATLANTIC OCEAN

U. OF
SOUTH
AFRICA

INDIAN

OCEAN

ARGENTINA

URUGUAY

BUENOS
AIRES

MONTEVIDEO

River Plate

CAPE TOWN

Cape of Good Hope

BATTLE OF THE
RIVER PLATE

Falkland I.

0   500   1000   1500

SCALE OF MILES

Cape Horn

THE SOUTH ATLANTIC

ately, one of Harwood's heavy cruisers was refitting at the Falkland Islands, and was unable to leave for another day.

The absence of this cruiser was serious, for it meant that Harwood had only six 8-inch guns on the heavy cruiser *Exeter*, eight 6-inch guns on the light cruiser *Achilles*, and the same number of 6-inch guns on the light cruiser *Ajax*. The *Graf Spee* carried six 11-inch guns and eight 5.9-inch guns. The total weight of the projectiles fired in one broadside from the *Graf Spee* was more than the total weight of those that could be fired at one time from all three British cruisers. Furthermore, the *Graf Spee's* 11-inch guns could fire almost 30,000 yards — nearly 18 miles — while the guns on the British ships could only fire about 20,000 yards, or less than 12 miles.

But Harwood and his squadron had prepared for such a battle. Even though they knew that they would be fighting at a handicap, they believed that by good teamwork they could beat the big German ship.

At dawn, on December 13, the three British cruisers were together, patrolling in the main sea-lanes off the River Plate. At 6:14 A.M. the British lookouts sighted smoke to the northeast. It was the German pocket battleship, less than twenty miles away. Harwood's hunch had been right. His careful calculations had even picked the exact day and place that the *Graf Spee* would appear.

The Battle of the River Plate

LANGSDORF saw the British ships almost as soon as they saw him, and he headed for them immediately. All ships were now going full speed, and so they approached each other at the rate of about 60 miles an hour. Three minutes after they had seen each other, Langsdorf opened fire, at more than 16 miles. Three minutes later, at ex-

20

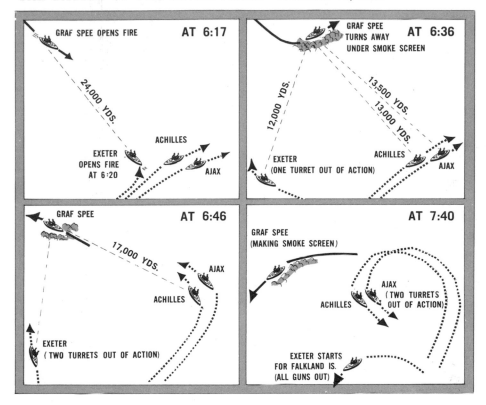

treme range, the *Exeter* began to return the fire. The first major sea battle of World War II had begun.

Langsdorf was a brave and skillful sea captain, but he had made a serious mistake. He had underestimated the courage, skill, and determination of his enemies. He should have stayed at long distance, out of range of the British guns, and hammered them. Instead, he rushed in to make a quick kill.

21

The *Graf Spee's* 11-inch guns began to score hits. Soon one of the three turrets on the *Exeter* was knocked out; at the same time the cruiser went out of control. The German ship now began to turn her fire to the two smaller cruisers, which were swinging wide, forcing the Germans to look and to shoot in three directions at once.

From the beginning of the fight the 8-inch and 6-inch guns of the *Exeter*, *Ajax*, and *Achilles* had been smashing into the German ship. Langsdorf realized that he was taking as much punishment as the British. Then he saw the damaged *Exeter* turn back into the fight, instead of running away, as he had expected.

Langsdorf was no coward, but he knew that there was no German base where he could get repairs. If the fight kept on the way it was going, he believed he could sink the three British ships. But his own vessel would be so badly damaged in such a fight to the finish that it would easily be overwhelmed by the next British warship to come along. And he had heard Harwood's radio message inviting the rest of the British navy to join in the fight.

The German captain decided, therefore, that he would try to get far enough from the British cruisers to batter them while they could not hit him. But he made this decision too late. Although the British ships were badly hit above the waterline, they still were able to steam as rapidly as the *Graf Spee*. Like dogs chasing a bear, they refused to let the German ship get out of range, no matter how she twisted and turned.

During all of this time the great shells were bursting on and around all four ships. The *Graf Spee* concentrated her fire on the *Exeter*. Finally, after an hour and twenty minutes of furious fighting, all of the *Exeter's* guns were knocked out. She was blazing furiously and close to sinking. Unable to keep up with the fight, the crippled *Exeter* turned away and limped slowly to the nearest British base in the Falkland Islands.

Commodore Harwood knew that he could not continue the daylight fight against the *Graf Spee*. Half of the guns on his own *Ajax* had been knocked out, and the *Achilles* was also badly hurt. He now turned away, to get out of range of the pocket battleship. He planned to follow, just out of reach of her big guns, and then to make another attack with guns and torpedoes after dark.

Langsdorf watched the British ships pull away, but he refused to follow. He realized the danger of a night battle, and he knew that the *Graf Spee* could not stand any more damage. He wanted to get repairs as quickly as possible, and he wanted to get his wounded men ashore. Hastily he turned his ship toward the nearest port, Montevideo, in neutral Uruguay. The two British light cruisers swung about and followed.

Late that night the *Graf Spee* sailed into Montevideo. The two battered British cruisers stayed just outside the Uruguayan territorial waters and made emergency repairs. They were still full of fight, and they felt that they had won the hard-fought battle. But they knew that if the *Graf Spee* came out again before British reinforcements arrived, they would be overwhelmed.

The End of the Graf Spee

THAT NIGHT and the next day Langsdorf made his own emergency repairs, and moved his wounded ashore. In vain he tried to get Uruguayan authorities to permit him to stay in port for dry-dock repairs. Under international law a ship at war could not stay in a neutral port for more than three days, and could not be permitted to receive help from neutral dockyards. The Uruguayan government insisted that if the *Graf Spee* did not leave within seventy-two hours

23

they would seize the ship under international law. The German captain reported the situation to Berlin by radio.

Late on December 14, while Langsdorf was arguing with the Uruguayans, the British heavy cruiser *Cumberland*, armed with eight 8-inch guns, arrived from the Falkland Islands. Commodore Harwood now felt that he could beat the *Graf Spee* if she tried to come out. Langsdorf thought so, too. And he knew from intercepted radio messages that two British aircraft carriers, and several more cruisers and destroyers, were less than 1,000 miles away, rushing to assist Harwood.

Early in the evening of December 16, just before sunset, the *Graf Spee* started to move slowly out of Montevideo. The seventy-two hours were almost up. "She's coming out!" the British lookouts shouted. The three cruisers prepared for action; the sailors waited tensely at their battle stations.

Suddenly, at the harbor entrance, there was a great explosion on the *Graf Spee*. Langsdorf had blown up his own ship. Before leaving the harbor he had put all of his crew, save for a few men, on a German merchant ship in the harbor.

As the pocket battleship sank to the bottom, Langsdorf and the remaining men on her got into lifeboats and returned to Montevideo. The German captain was heartbroken. He had decided against renewing the battle because he could not bear to see more of his men killed in a hopeless fight. Hitler himself had approved the decision. But Langsdorf felt that he had dishonored himself by refusing to fight. Three days later he shot himself.

Rather than deliver it into British hands, Captain Langsdorf of the Graf Spee *blew up his own ship just outside of the harbor at Montevideo.*

The War Gets Hotter

The "Phony War"

AFTER THE BATTLE of the River Plate, the war at sea settled down to the routine of blockade, submarine attacks, and convoy operations. It was hard, tense, dangerous work; ships and submarines on both sides were sunk; the lists of men killed and wounded mounted. But as the destruction continued, day after day, week after week, into the early months of 1940, it became, even to the

25

men who were engaged in it, almost dull.

On land, meanwhile, there had been little action since the Germans had overwhelmed Poland. French and British troops sat in the Maginot Line and in the trenches along the border of Belgium and wondered if they were really in a war. They trained and marched and drilled. But even though the French and German soldiers could see each other clearly along the border between their two countries, there was no fighting. This strange interval was called the "phony war."

The Altmark *Affair*

THE MOST exciting incident during this "phony war" period came in a very small naval action in Norwegian territorial waters.

In February, 1940, the British learned that the supply ship *Altmark*, carrying the 300 British prisoners who had been captured by the *Graf Spee,* had reached northern Norway. And they found out that the *Altmark* was working its way southward, down the long Norwegian coast, always careful to stay within three miles of land, and stopping every night deep in some Norwegian fjord or inlet.

Norway was neutral, and so British warships were not permitted under international law to attack an enemy ship in Norwegian territorial waters. But the British were certain that the *Altmark* herself was violating international law, which also says that no armed ship of a nation at war can stay in a neutral country's waters for more than seventy-two hours. If the *Altmark* had any guns on board—and the British were certain she did—then the Norwegians should not allow her to sneak down their coast.

Churchill, accordingly, ordered Captain Philip Vian, in command of a destroyer squadron, to rescue the British sailors, even if this meant using force against Norwegian armed interference.

Vian, discovering that the *Altmark* was anchored deep inside Jossing Fjord, sailed into Norwegian waters in his destroyer, HMS *Cossack*, and entered the fjord past two protesting Norwegian gunboats. When the Norwegian sailors saw that Vian meant business, they did not shoot, but continued to protest by radio.

When the captain of the *Altmark* saw the *Cossack* steaming toward him, he tried to ram the British vessel. Vian immediately pulled his destroyer alongside the German ship and, while part of his crew lashed the two vessels together, he directed his men to board the enemy ship. The men swarmed over the rail to board the *Altmark*, and the Germans fought back. It was a sea fight with cutlasses and pistols, just like those that took place in the days of sailing vessels.

Despite fierce German resistance, the British tars soon cleared the *Altmark's* decks. They found the prisoners and took them on board the *Cossack*. Meanwhile, they had discovered that the *Altmark* carried two light cannons and four machine guns. When Norway protested the British violation of Norwegian neutrality, Great Britain protested that the Norwegians themselves had violated international law by permitting the armed *Altmark* to stay in their waters. Vian, the *Cossack,* and the released prisoners returned to England in triumph.

Eyes on Norway

MOST of the iron ore used in German war production came from northern Sweden. Nearly all of it was shipped by rail to the Norwegian port of Narvik, then sent in cargo boats down the coasts of Norway and Denmark, always within the three-mile limit, to Ger-

NORWAY AND NORTH SEA

NORTH CAPE

ICELAND

Altaljord

TROMSOE

NARVIK

U.S.S.R.

0   100   200   300
Scale of Miles

NORWEGIAN

SEA

IRON ORE
R.R.

ATLANTIC OCEAN

LULEA

Faeroe Is.

TRONDHEIM

FINLAND

Scapa Flow

BERGEN

NORWAY

OSLO

STOCKHOLM

SCOTLAND

STAVANGER

Jossing Fjord

SWEDEN

EST.

KRISTIANSAND

Skagerrak

BALTIC SEA

KATTEGAT

LATVIA

NORTH SEA

Denmark

LITHUANIA

CUXHAVEN

SWINEMUNDE

WILHELMSHAVEN

KIEL

ENGLAND

CANAL

GDYNIA

LONDON

Dover

NETH.

GERMANY

POLAND

Strait of

DUNKIRK

BELG.

FRANCE

many. Under international law there was nothing the British could do about this.

At the same time, however, the Germans were using Norwegian waters illegally, as was shown by the *Altmark* incident. The German navy usually sent its surface raiders close to the coast in bad weather so that they could sneak out past the British blockade. If the Norwegians knew this, they were probably afraid to protest to Germany. They answered British protests by saying that their patrol boats had never seen the German raiders. This was true, of course, for the Germans always waited for bad weather when they could not be seen.

Hitler had already decided that the iron ore from Sweden was so important to Germany that he would have to seize Norway and Denmark in order to prevent the British from interfering with the shipments. He also realized that if the long Norwegian coast was under German control, the British would have a much more difficult time enforcing their blockade. The *Altmark* affair made Hitler decide to go ahead as quickly as possible with his plan to invade the two Scandinavian countries.

The same incident also convinced the British that they must do something to block Norwegian territorial waters to German warships. If this also blocked the shipments of iron ore to Germany, they would not mind at all. They decided to lay minefields right up to the coast of Norway, within the three-mile limit.

Germany Invades Norway

ON APRIL 8, 1940, there occurred one of the amazing coincidences of the war. The Royal Navy began to lay its minefields off the coast of Norway just as the German navy arrived to cover the carefully

29

planned German invasion of that country. All that day a series of sharp naval actions between British destroyers and the German navy took place along the Norwegian coast.

In one of the memorable actions of the war, the British destroyer HMS *Glowworm* suddenly found herself in the middle of a strong German squadron. After taking heavy punishment, the *Glowworm* charged directly at the German heavy cruiser *Hipper*. The *Hipper* tried to turn away, but the *Glowworm* rammed her, tearing a great hole in her side. Immediately afterward the British destroyer blew up with all on board, but she had accomplished her mission; the *Hipper*, close to sinking, was forced to limp back to Germany.

The German heavy cruiser Hipper *at Kiel for repairs after having been rammed by the British destroyer HMS* Glowworm.

Now realizing that Germany was actually invading Norway, the main forces of the British navy rushed to interfere. On April 9, and again the next day, they engaged the Germans in a number of short but fierce running battles along the coast of Norway. The British battle cruiser, HMS *Renown,* damaged the *Gneisenau*; two other German cruisers were sunk, and the pocket battleship *Lutzow* was damaged by British surface ships and submarines. But though the British had the best of most of these encounters, they had arrived one day too late. The Germans had successfully completed their first landings.

The invasion of Norway had not been as easy as the Germans may have anticipated. At Oslo Fjord three small Norwegian gunboats, supported by strong shore batteries, had faced up to two German cruisers, several destroyers, and some smaller vessels. The three Norwegian ships had succeeded in sinking one German cruiser and a minesweeper, and had damaged the other cruiser and two destroyers before they were themselves sunk by the Germans.

Norwegian resistance had not ended with the sinking of the brave little gunboats. Presently the Germans were forced to withdraw in the face of accurate fire from Norwegian shore batteries. Oslo was finally captured by a German airborne attack after the naval assault had been driven off. Meanwhile, five other Norwegian ports had been captured by the Germans: Narvik, Trondheim, Bergen, Stavanger, and Kristiansand.

Now German air units moved into the captured Norwegian airfields and immediately began violent attacks on British warships off the coast. After suffering severe damage from these air attacks, the Royal Navy had to pull away from the coast of southern Norway, but two more fierce naval actions took place in northern Norwegian waters, where narrow Narvik Fjord extends more than forty miles inland to the town of Narvik.

The German landing force that had captured Narvik had been convoyed by ten German destroyers and one submarine. Because of the concentration of the British fleet off the coast, these German warships had remained in the fjord, where the British could not easily attack them. At the same time, their guns would help the German soldiers to defend Narvik from any Allied attempts to recapture the town.

On April 10 a force of five British destroyers, commanded by Captain Warburton-Lee, boldly sailed up the narrow fjord. They caught

British troops returning from the Lofoten Islands off Norway, where they blew up tanks containing oil destined for German ships.

PHOTO FROM EUROPEAN

five of the German destroyers by surprise, sank two, and damaged the others. The other five German destroyers then entered the battle. The British inflicted severe damage on the German ships, but finally the British ships were forced to withdraw. Two British vessels had been sunk, and two more damaged in the fight.

Three days later the British battleship *Warspite*, with nine destroyers, steamed up the fjord. Despite heavy artillery fire from the German troops in Narvik, the British ships quickly sank the remaining eight German destroyers and the submarine.

The Allies now tried to help Norway by sending two small army expeditions to recapture Trondheim and Narvik from the Germans. An Anglo-French force, 30,000 strong, landed north and south of Trondheim in mid-April, but was soon driven back by German counterattacks supported by overwhelming air superiority. At the beginning of May, less than three weeks after they had landed, the Allies were forced to get back on their ships and return to England.

Despite their defeat in central Norway, the British succeeded in landing troops near Narvik. After tough fighting in deep snow, they captured the town on May 28. By this time, however, the German victories in Flanders and France had completely changed the course of the war. Early in June the Allies withdrew from Narvik.

The final naval action off the coast of Norway came on June 8, as the battle cruisers *Gneisenau* and *Scharnhorst* tried to reach the British transports carrying the soldiers away from Narvik. They surprised the British aircraft carrier *Glorious*, which was accompanied by two destroyers. The captain of the *Glorious* was sure that there were no German ships nearby, and so he had made the amazing mistake of not having his scouting planes up in the air. He did not even have any planes on the flight deck ready to take off. Before a single plane could get in the air, the aircraft carrier was sunk by the

German ships. The two British destroyers bravely attacked the battle cruisers but they, too, were quickly sunk in the unequal battle — though not before one of them had severely damaged the *Scharnhorst* with a torpedo. A few days later the *Gneisenau* was hit by a torpedo from a British submarine, so both of the German battle cruisers were out of action for six months.

The "Miracle of Dunkirk"

ON MAY 10, 1940, German armies poured over the frontiers of Belgium and Holland and into France. Within ten days the Germans had overwhelmed the initial Allied defenses and had struck through northern France to reach the English Channel. More than 1,000,000 Allied soldiers — including some 300,000 British and about the same number of Belgians — had been cut off from the main French armies in France.

Because of this terrible Allied disaster, Britain had turned to Winston Churchill to lead the country as Prime Minister. The wise and strong-willed man knew that the situation was desperate, and that France and Britain were both in danger of being completely destroyed by Hitler. But he never lost heart. Confident in the rightness of his cause, and in the strength and determination of his people, he never doubted that Britain would win in the end. The English people responded magnificently to his leadership.

Meanwhile, the German net tightened around the Allied troops cut off in northern France and Belgium. The Royal Navy and the Royal Air Force entered the battle in an effort to hold back the Germans long enough so that a few of the surrounded men could escape by sea. The task became harder when Belgium surrendered and the British troops were pushed back to the sea at Dunkirk.

While the RAF successfully challenged German supremacy in the skies, the British navy moved in all its available destroyers and small naval ships toward Dunkirk. (Larger ships could not get close enough to shore to rescue the waiting soldiers.) The warships were joined by every kind of British vessel imaginable. Every Englishman who owned a boat, or who could help to sail one, volunteered to help. There were tugboats, fishing boats, private yachts, motorboats, sailboats, ferryboats — anything that could go on the water, and that was big enough to reach Dunkirk from the English coast.

Between May 28 and June 4 the Royal Navy, with its civilian helpers, carried more than 338,000 British, French, and Belgian soldiers from Dunkirk to England — more than six times as many as they had expected to save when the operation started. There had been 861 vessels of all kinds taking part in this great national effort. Of these, 243 had been sunk, and many of the rest had been damaged one way or another. But the job was done, and most of the British army had been saved.

The Dark Days of 1940

The Shifting Balance of Sea Power

LESS than four weeks after Dunkirk, France surrendered to Hitler. Now everyone expected the German army to invade England. Few people outside of Britain thought that such an invasion could be repulsed, but Churchill and his people believed that their navy and air force would stop the Germans if they tried to cross the English Channel. Moreover, nearly 300,000 trained, veteran soldiers, brought back from the beaches of Dunkirk, stood ready to fight on the beaches

35

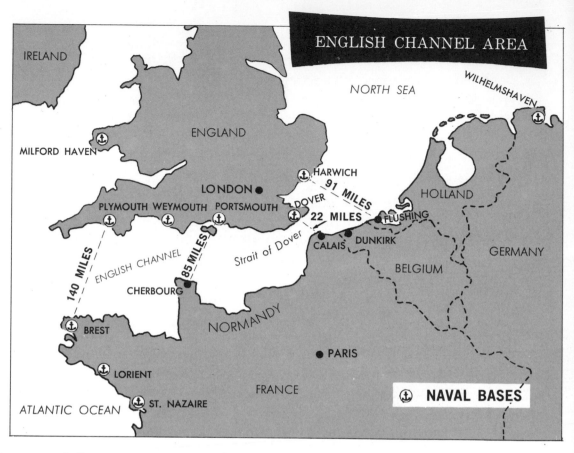

ENGLISH CHANNEL AREA

IRELAND

NORTH SEA

WILHELMSHAVEN

ENGLAND

MILFORD HAVEN

HARWICH

91 MILES

LONDON

HOLLAND

PLYMOUTH WEYMOUTH PORTSMOUTH

DOVER

22 MILES

FLUSHING

140 MILES

ENGLISH CHANNEL

85 MILES

Strait of Dover

CALAIS

DUNKIRK

GERMANY

CHERBOURG

BELGIUM

BREST

NORMANDY

LORIENT

PARIS

FRANCE

NAVAL BASES

ATLANTIC OCEAN

ST. NAZAIRE

of their own country if the Germans managed to get any troops on English soil. This alone made the evacuation of Dunkirk worth whatever it had cost.

The cost of the evacuation had been very heavy. Six British destroyers had been sunk, and nineteen had been damaged and put temporarily out of action. Even before Dunkirk there had not been enough British destroyers to do a really efficient job of protecting merchant ship convoys, keeping up the blockade of Germany, and operating with the main fleets. To make things worse, the conquests of Norway and France had given Germany more naval bases, alarmingly close to Atlantic sea-lanes. The British needed destroyers more than ever before for blockade and convoy duty.

On top of this, Italy had entered the war on June 10. This meant that the strong Italian fleet was added to that of Germany. The British had counted on the French fleet to help them offset the Italians in the Mediterranean, but the French navy had left the war, and the British could not even be sure that it would not be taken over by the Germans. The Italian navy by itself was much stronger than the British Mediterranean fleet, and Churchill could not spare any more ships to send to the Mediterranean.

Although the shortage of destroyers was very serious, Churchill hoped that the Royal Navy could manage somehow to hold its own against the German and Italian fleets until February, 1941. At that time 20 new British destroyers and 60 corvettes (small destroyers) would be completed, in addition to many other small patrol vessels. Churchill had started work on all of these just as soon as he became First Lord of the Admiralty at the outset of the war.

Worst of all, from the British point of view, was the danger that the whole French fleet might fall into Hitler's hands. If that happened, then there was probably nothing that Churchill or anyone else could do to keep British shipping from being swept off the seas by combined submarine, surface, and air attack.

The French Fleet

AT THE TIME France surrendered to Germany, the French fleet was distributed in several locations. Two battleships, four cruisers, eight destroyers, some submarines and a number of smaller vessels were in English ports. The strongest French fleet was at Oran, in Algeria.

This fleet consisted of four battleships, several cruisers, destroyers, submarines, and smaller vessels. At Alexandria, in Egypt, there was a squadron of one battleship, four cruisers, and three destroyers, attached to the British Mediterranean fleet. In addition there were a number of cruisers at Algiers and at the naval base of Toulon in southern France, and a few others were scattered in French overseas possessions. Two powerful new battleships, almost completed in French shipyards at the time of the surrender, had sailed to Africa. The *Jean Bart*, with no guns, had taken refuge in the Moroccan port of Casablanca. The *Richelieu* was farther down the African coast at Dakar.

The British government decided that it must take steps to see that as few of these ships as possible should ever come under Hitler's control.

Early on July 3 the British seized all French ships that were anchored in English ports. Almost all of the crews willingly joined the Free French forces under General Charles de Gaulle, and fought bravely beside the British throughout the rest of the war.

At Alexandria, Admiral Sir Andrew Cunningham, in command of the British Eastern Mediterranean fleet, persuaded the French admiral to disarm his vessels. Cunningham did much of his persuading by pointing the big guns of the British fleet at the French warships.

That same morning a British squadron of three battleships, an aircraft carrier, two cruisers, and eleven destroyers arrived off the French naval base at Oran. Vice Admiral James Somerville gave the French squadron there three choices: (1) to join the English and continue the fight against Germany; (2) to sail to England or some other agreed upon place and permit the ships to be disarmed until the end of the war; or (3) to sink their own ships in Oran harbor.

British aircraft carrier HMS Ark Royal, *from whose decks air attacks were launched against French ships at Oran.*

Somerville told the French admiral that if he did not do one of these things, he was under orders from the British government to attack and destroy the French fleet.

The French admiral insisted that he would never turn the French ships over to the Italians or the Germans, but he refused to agree to Somerville's terms. The British were most reluctant to start a fight with their recent allies, but they knew that the survival of their nation might be at stake. When the French continued to refuse repeated requests to accept the terms, Somerville finally opened fire.

The battle was a short one. The bombardment by the British

battleships *Hood, Valiant,* and *Resolution* was followed by air attacks launched from the carrier *Ark Royal.* Three of the French battleships were sunk, or run aground. One escaped, and with five destroyers reached Toulon. The British suffered no serious damage from the French ships or from the shore batteries.

Five days later at Dakar the *Richelieu* also refused to surrender to the English. She was seriously damaged by an air strike from the British carrier *Hermes,* and by explosive charges placed against her side in a daring motor torpedo boat attack.

These actions naturally embittered most Frenchmen against their former allies. They could not understand why the British would strike them so hard in the moment of their great sorrow after defeat by Germany. But, though it took a long time for these bitter feelings to change, the British had accomplished what they felt was necessary for their own survival. What remained of the French fleet was so small that it could never be of great help to the Germans and Italians.

Objective: Britain

ON JULY 16, 1940, Hitler ordered his generals and admirals to prepare for an invasion of Britain. The German military staffs promptly got together and worked out the plans for Operation "Sea Lion," which provided for landings on the southeast coast of England beginning September 28.

Neither the German army nor the German navy was very happy about this. They did not think there was time enough to make all of the preparations, nor to gather together enough boats to carry the soldiers across the English Channel. Also, they were afraid that British air and naval attacks would not only interfere with the preparations, but would also sink so many of the invasion ships during the crossing that the landings would fail.

40

But the German *Luftwaffe*, under Hermann Goering, assured the soldiers and sailors that they would destroy the British air force before September, and would then drive the Royal Navy away from southeast England, in the same way they had earlier cleared it from the waters of southern Norway. German sailors who had fought the Englishmen had some doubts about this, but they watched to see what Goering's airmen could do.

A civilian volunteer watches the skies above London for approaching German aircraft during the Battle of Britain.

WIDE WORLD PHOTO

American sailors show two British sailors how depth charges are laid from one of the fifty over-age United States destroyers traded to Great Britain by the United States in return for naval and air bases.

In July the German air force began intensive attacks against the airfields and seaports of southern England. This was the beginning of the Battle of Britain between the *Luftwaffe* and the Royal Air Force. All through July and August the battle raged over the skies of the English Channel and England. By early September it was clear to everyone that the British had won the battle. The Germans had been unable to gain control of the air, and were losing about twice as many planes as the British. Everyone now knew that the *Luftwaffe* would not be able to stop British air and naval attacks against the invasion armada. On September 14 Hitler canceled Operation "Sea Lion."

A Success and a Failure

DESPITE their victory in the Battle of Britain, the British were still losing destroyers in their unending battles with German submarines and airplanes on the merchant sea-lanes approaching Britain. Churchill worried more and more about what might happen before February, 1941, when the first new destroyers would be ready.

In early September, however, Churchill reached a momentous agreement with President Roosevelt of the United States. The American government agreed to give Britain fifty of its old destroyers, in return for bases on British possessions in the Western Hemisphere. This meant that Britain could keep up its convoy protection and its blockade during the winter. It also meant that the United States would be able to use bases on British islands to protect the approaches to American waters in case she, too, went to war with Germany.

With these additional destroyers quickly arriving to reinforce the British fleet, Churchill approved an operation which would make the South Atlantic sea-lanes safer. The British government had been afraid that the Germans would use the French port of Dakar, near the narrowest part of the South Atlantic, as a submarine and raider base. General de Gaulle, furthermore, was anxious to liberate some important French colonial city from the control of the Vichy government. So it was agreed that a Free French force, commanded by de Gaulle himself, and supported by a combined Free French-British naval squadron, would seize Dakar.

A combination of Allied mistakes and bad luck, however, made it possible for the Vichy French to reinforce Dakar with three cruisers and three destroyers just before the Allied force arrived off the coast. Bad weather hampered the bombardment of shore defenses and the landing of Free French troops. In addition, the Vichy French defenders fought so determinedly that Churchill decided to call off the attack, rather than add to the bitterness already existing between Vichy France and England.

The Naval Struggle for the Mediterranean

Early Engagements

THE FIRST action in the Mediterranean war came on June 11, 1940, the day after Mussolini declared war against France and Britain. Two waves of Italian planes bombed the British naval base at Malta — a tiny island only 55 miles away from Sicily. This was the first of thousands of attacks that Malta would endure for more than three years.

THE MEDITERRANEAN

Although British squadrons several times approached the coast
of Italy there was no engagement between surface forces until
July 9. That day Admiral Sir Andrew Cunningham had most of his
Eastern Mediterranean fleet out to protect convoys carrying supplies
to Malta and evacuating British families from the island. He had
three battleships, an aircraft carrier, five light cruisers, and a number
of destroyers. East of Sicily, and south of Calabria (the toe of the
Italian boot), the British ran across an Italian squadron of two
battleships, six heavy cruisers, twelve light cruisers, and a number
of destroyers. The Italians were returning from escorting a troop

45

convoy to Benghazi, in the Italian North African colony of Tripoli.

The British immediately attacked, but the faster Italian ships quickly headed for the coast of Calabria. In the running fight that followed, the Italians were supported by a number of land-based Italian planes, but no serious damage was done to the British ships. One Italian battleship and a cruiser were badly damaged, but by this time they had come so close to the Italian coast that the British fleet had to turn away.

Ten days later the Australian light cruiser HMS *Sydney*, accompanied by four destroyers, became engaged with two Italian light cruisers off the northwestern coast of Crete. The *Sydney* sank the fast Italian cruiser *Bartolomeo Colleoni*, but the other Italian vessel was able to escape to Tobruk.

During the late summer and fall the British reinforced Malta and improved its defenses. Naval units also supported the British army in clashes along the coast near the Libya-Egypt frontier. In October, HMS *Ajax* — of River Plate fame — sank two Italian destroyers and severely damaged another.

The Attack on Taranto

THE ITALIAN NAVY had not gone to sea in any strength after the July battle off Calabria. But Admiral Cunningham was worried by the concentration of all six Italian battleships, and most of the remainder of the Italian fleet, in Taranto harbor. This fleet was considerably larger than his total strength in the Mediterranean. He therefore decided to carry the fight to the Italian fleet in the harbor.

On the night of November 11 the British Mediterranean fleet secretly approached the south Italian coast. Twelve airplanes armed with torpedoes were launched from the carrier HMS *Illustrious*,

46

The battleship Conte di Cavour *with its sister battleship* Littorio, *both prides of the Italian navy.*

and headed for Taranto. While some more planes from the *Illustrious* dropped flares to light up the harbor, and others attacked the antiaircraft defenses of the harbor, the twelve attack planes headed for the Italian battleships. Flying at low level, through a storm of antiaircraft fire from the shore and from the fleet, these planes hit four of the battleships, a cruiser, and a destroyer. Three battleships were run aground in sinking condition. The other three ships were damaged. Two British planes were shot down. This, however, was a small price to pay for what had been gained. The attack had assured the British of naval supremacy over the Italians in the Mediterranean. The damaged Italian battleships were repaired before March, but it would be many months before the other three would be ready to fight again.

German Intervention in the Mediterranean

IN JANUARY, 1941, British superiority in the Mediterranean was challenged by the Germans. The *Luftwaffe's* Tenth Air Fleet, with 500 planes, was transferred from Norway to southern Italy and Sicily. This was the German air unit which had driven British ships from the Norwegian coast in April, 1940. In mid-January the Germans sank a British cruiser, and so seriously damaged the carrier *Illustrious* that she had to be sunk.

From that time on the Germans made it very difficult for the British to maintain their supply line from Gibraltar to Malta to Alexandria. Most British supply ships to the Middle East were forced to go all the way around Africa to Egypt by way of the Red Sea. At the same time, the British fleet was forced to fight off incessant, and frequently damaging, air attacks.

Despite German air superiority, on February 9 Admiral Somerville, with two battleships, an aircraft carrier and a cruiser, carried out a daring and highly damaging bombardment of Genoa and other ports along the northwest coast of Italy. The entire Italian fleet, supported by German and Italian planes, came out to try to catch Somerville and his ships. But the British got away untouched.

Battle of Cape Matapan

In March the British began to send a small army from Egypt to Greece, to meet an expected German invasion of that little country. Upon the urging of the Germans, the Italians sent out their fleet in an effort to intercept the British troop convoys. Late in March all three seaworthy Italian battleships, under the command of Admiral Angelo Iachino, sailed into the Eastern Mediterranean. In the lead the fast and powerful battleship *Vittorio Veneto*, accompanied by three cruisers and several destroyers, cruised south of Crete. At the same time five cruisers and a number of destroyers swept the waters between Crete and Cape Matapan, on the Greek mainland. The remaining two battleships and supporting ships were between southern Italy and Greece. All three portions of the Italian fleet were covered by German and Italian planes.

On March 27 a British patrol plane discovered the two leading Italian forces near Crete and reported that they were approaching two large British troop convoys. Admiral Cunningham immediately ordered the convoys to return to port, while he took his fleet out to find the enemy. His total force consisted of three battleships, one carrier, four cruisers, and more than a dozen destroyers.

Early on March 28 the British cruiser squadron became engaged with the *Vittorio Veneto's* squadron. The British cruisers immediately turned back to try to lure the Italians within range of the

British battleships, which were still 90 miles away. At the same time British carrier planes began to attack the Italians.

Before noon the Italians turned away, still more than 50 miles from the British battleships. Admiral Cunningham pursued them while his carrier planes continued the attacks to try to slow down the Italian withdrawal. Shortly after 3:00 P.M. the *Vittorio Veneto* was hit by a torpedo, and was forced to slow down her speed considerably. Just before dark the British carrier's planes also hit and stopped the heavy cruiser *Pola*.

The British continued their pursuit during the night, though they were slightly deceived by a change in the direction of the Italian fleet. On the other hand, the Italians apparently did not expect the British to follow so closely as they did. After dark, Admiral Iachino sent back two cruisers and four destroyers to assist the damaged *Pola*.

By about 10:00 P.M. the main British fleet had almost reached the *Pola*, just as the returning Italian ships were approaching. Since all the ships were dark, they failed at first to see each other. Then suddenly the British sighted the Italian ships. The three British battleships turned all their heavy guns on the unsuspecting Italians, less than three miles away, while a British destroyer illuminated them with a searchlight. In a few seconds the two Italian cruisers and two of the accompanying destroyers were blazing wrecks. Soon after this the helpless *Pola* was discovered. The British removed her crew as prisoners, and sank her. By that time it was after midnight, and Cunningham realized that the main Italian fleet had escaped. He was disappointed that the *Vittorio Veneto* and other damaged Italian ships had gotten away. He had, however, gained a substantial victory in sinking five Italian vessels, while only one British cruiser had been slightly damaged and one airplane had been lost. Still more important was the fact that after the Battle of Cape Matapan the

Italian fleet rarely again came out in force any distance from the safety of the coast of Italy. It spent most of the rest of the war in the harbor of La Spezia, as far away from the British fleet as it could get.

Greece and Crete

ON APRIL 6, 1940, the German army launched a violent attack against Greece and Yugoslavia. It quickly overwhelmed Yugoslavia and soon after, forced the Greek army to surrender. British troops in Greece had to try to escape by sea. As at Dunkirk, the Royal Navy was standing by to do its best, but this time the Royal Air Force was not there to support it in the sky. Thus the British warships and troop transports could approach the coast only after dark, and had to leave in time to be well on their way before dawn.

Despite these handicaps and despite constant pummeling from the air, the Royal Navy evacuated over 50,000 troops from Greece during night operations from April 24 to April 29. A total of 26 ships — including two destroyers — were lost to the German dive bombers. A number of other warships and transports were damaged.

The next German objective was the island of Crete. Moving in powerful air force units to fields in Greece, the Germans were soon hammering Crete and harassing Admiral Cunningham's ships in the waters around the island. Beginning on May 20 the Germans began an airborne attack on Crete — the first time that airborne troops had been used on so large a scale.

Admiral Cunningham's fleet immediately went into action. The next nine days saw the most intensive, most prolonged fight that has ever taken place between a fleet and a powerful land-based air force.

51

On the night of May 21-22, British squadrons patrolling between Crete and Greece discovered two convoys of small boats carrying German troops to the assistance of their airborne comrades already fighting on Crete. The British warships attacked immediately and sank a number of the small boats, killing 5,000 German soldiers. At least an equal number escaped back to Greece, however. The British ships were running out of antiaircraft ammunition and they had to turn away or risk being caught by German aircraft at dawn off the Greek coast.

The next day was one of the worst the Royal Navy ever experienced. In continuous battles with German aircraft all around Crete, Cunningham lost two cruisers and a destroyer, while two of his battleships and two more cruisers were severely damaged. Reluctantly he decided that he would have to keep his ships south of Crete during daylight hours, while continuing night patrols to keep the Germans from sending reinforcements by sea.

In the next few days the Germans began to gain the upper hand on Crete, while the British fleet continued to take heavy punishment from the *Luftwaffe*. Another battleship, an aircraft carrier, and several smaller ships were damaged. It soon became obvious that further resistance on Crete was impossible.

But now there was a serious question whether the Royal Navy should risk further serious losses in order to try to evacuate as many soldiers as possible from Crete. Even Churchill was reluctant to order the battered ships and exhausted sailors to make another dangerous, and possibly useless, effort. Admiral Cunningham soon settled the matter. "Stick it out," he said to his men, in a radio message to the fleet. "We must never let the Army down."

They did not. Losses in men and ships were heavy during the two awful days and night of May 28 and May 29. But slightly more than 16,000 Allied soldiers were brought back to Alexandria — about half of those who had started the battle.

British naval losses were appalling. Four cruisers and six destroyers had been sunk. One carrier and three battleships had been damaged — the carrier and two of the battleships so seriously that they would be out of action for months. Several other cruisers and destroyers had also been badly damaged. More than 2,000 British sailors had been killed.

The Raiders

The Scheer *and the* Jervis Bay

LATE IN OCTOBER, 1940, the pocket battleship *Admiral Scheer,* commanded by Captain Theodore Krancke, slipped past the British patrols and began to prowl the North Atlantic shipping lanes. Late in the afternoon of November 5, she encountered a large British convoy of 37 merchant ships protected only by the armed merchant cruiser *Jervis Bay,* which carried four old six-inch guns.

As soon as Captain E. F. S. Fegen of the *Jervis Bay* sighted the German battleship, he reported his finding by urgent radio to the British Admiralty and ordered the ships of his convoy to scatter. Then, though he knew the fight would be hopeless, Fegen steamed directly toward the powerful pocket battleship, which immediately opened fire. By skillful maneuvering, Fegen prolonged the unequal fight for an hour before his ship began to sink. He himself was killed, but he had accomplished at least part of his mission. By the time the fight was over, night had fallen, and in the darkness the *Scheer* was

German battle cruisers Gneisenau *and* Scharnhorst *preyed on British convoys in the Atlantic. At one time they sank sixteen ships in two days.*

able to find and sink only five of the helpless merchant ships: thirty-two got away.

The German captain was disappointed that he had not been able to do more damage to the British convoy, but he, too, had accomplished part of his mission. For a week the British held up all their North Atlantic convoys. When the convoys were resumed, the British were forced to send with each convoy a battleship or several cruisers, plus destroyers.

Hipper, Scharnhorst *and* Gneisenau

WHILE KRANCKE and the *Scheer* continued their destructive raids through the South Atlantic and the Indian Ocean, three other large German ships slipped past the thin line of British patrol ships to reach the North Atlantic. The first of these was the heavy cruiser *Hipper,* who began her raid in November. She was not successful at first because by then all the British convoys were heavily protected by large warships — the result of the *Scheer's* raid.

Engine trouble forced the *Hipper* to stop for repairs in the French port of Brest, but in February she returned to the sea-lanes and sank seven British ships in two weeks. Then, after another repair stop at Brest, she returned to Germany in April, evading British patrols between Iceland and Scotland, just as the *Scheer* had done a short time earlier.

Meanwhile, late in January, 1941, German Vice Admiral Günther Lütjens took the battle cruisers *Gneisenau* and *Scharnhorst* out as a raiding squadron. For over a month they, too, were unable to find British convoys unprotected by battleships, though they did sink five unescorted merchant ships. On March 15, however, the raiders found a convoy that was just scattering from a submarine attack. In two days the German battle cruisers sank sixteen ships. Then, as British battleships raced to the area, the two raiders sped to safety in Brest. Here, however, British bomber planes found them, and damaged both German ships so badly that they were out of action for several months.

The Cruise of the Bismarck *and the* Prinz Eugen

EARLY IN 1941 the Germans completed a new battleship, the *Bismarck.* She carried eight 15-inch guns, twelve 5.9-inch guns, sixteen

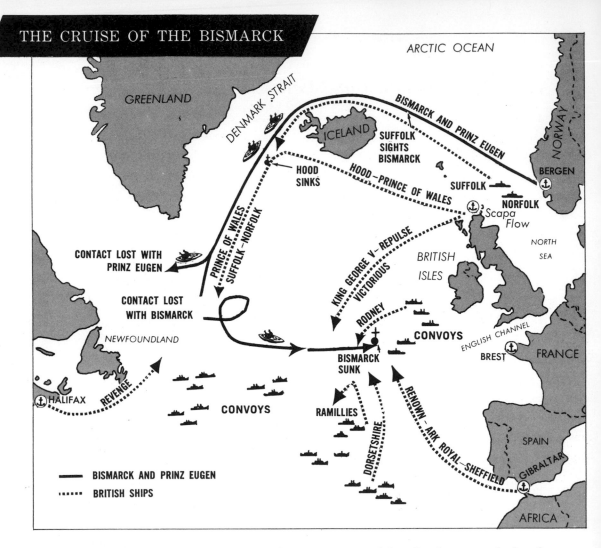

4.1-inch antiaircraft guns, and was protected by the heaviest belt of armor ever put on a battleship up to that time. Despite this weight, her powerful engines would carry her at 30 knots — as fast as most battle cruisers and cruisers. In addition, she had numerous watertight compartments which, in combination with her armor, made her as close to unsinkable as any vessel has ever been. In May, 1941, she was the most powerful single warship in the world.

56

At about the same time the Germans also completed a new heavy cruiser, the *Prinz Eugen*, carrying eight 8-inch guns, plus a secondary armament of 5.9-inch and 4.1-inch guns. Though her guns were smaller, this ship was heavier and faster than the pocket battleships, and considerably more powerful than any British heavy cruiser.

The German naval staff now planned to send the *Bismarck* and the *Prinz Eugen* on a raid into the Atlantic, where they would be joined by the *Scharnhorst* and the *Gneisenau*. But the success of British air attacks on the battle cruisers in Brest forced the Germans to abandon this plan. Accordingly, Admiral Lütjens came back to Germany to take the *Bismarck* and the *Prinz Eugen* out by themselves.

On May 18, 1941, the two German ships sailed from the captured Polish naval base at Gdynia. Lütjens took his ships into Norwegian waters, where he took refuge in Bergen Fjord until he could take advantage of foggy or stormy weather to slip past the blockade. British reconnaissance planes found the German ships there on May 21.

At Scapa Flow, Admiral Sir John Tovey, commanding the Home Fleet, had only one fully operational modern battleship — his flagship, HMS *King George V*, with ten 14-inch guns, but not so well protected as the *Bismarck*, and not quite so fast. He also had her sister ship, HMS *Prince of Wales*, a brand-new vessel with a brand-new crew, and still having trouble with some "bugs" in her machinery. Actually the *Bismarck* was just as new, but was much more ready for battle.

In addition, Tovey had the old, but fast, battle cruiser HMS *Hood*, the largest ship in the Royal Navy, carrying eight 15-inch guns, and probably the only large British ship as fast as the *Bismarck*. But the *Hood*, like all battle cruisers, had less armor than the usual battleship; she was built to hit hard and run fast, but not to take much punishment.

To be ready for the *Bismarck*, provided the German vessel should get past the cruiser and destroyer patrols, Tovey sent the *Hood* and the *Prince of Wales*, along with some destroyers, to take position south of Iceland. There they would be ready to intercept the German ships whether they came out through Denmark Strait, or west of the Faeroes. He kept the *King George V*, with several cruisers and destroyers, at Scapa Flow, ready to sail as soon as the German ships made a move.

Actually, under the cover of fog, Lütjens had taken his vessels out of Bergen harbor late on May 21. British reconnaissance planes did not discover this until the following afternoon. Tovey immediately alerted the *Hood* and *Prince of Wales*, and took to sea with the *King George V*, heading westward toward Iceland. The Admiralty reinforced him with the new aircraft carrier *Victorious*, and the old battle cruiser HMS *Repulse*.

Meanwhile the two German ships had been heading for Denmark Strait, which they reached late on May 23. Shortly before dusk the patrolling cruiser HMS *Suffolk* caught sight of the Germans, and was soon joined by her patrol-mate, HMS *Norfolk*. Keeping just out of range, the two British cruisers stayed right behind the German ships, holding contact with them by means of their effective new radar sets.

At this time there were more British convoys than usual on the North Atlantic. One of these was a troop convoy, carrying several thousand men as reinforcements to the Middle East. The *Repulse* and the *Victorious* had originally been scheduled to accompany them. To make sure that the precious convoy would not be intercepted by the German raiders, the Admiralty ordered Admiral Somerville to steam north from Gibraltar as soon as possible with his

58

PHOTO FROM U.S. NAVY DEPARTMENT, #80-G-13353, IN THE NATIONAL ARCHIVES

An Allied convoy makes its way through storm and fog off Iceland.

Force H, which at that time consisted only of the battle cruiser *Renown*, the carrier *Ark Royal*, the cruiser *Sheffield*, and a few destroyers. Somerville, expecting the order, was on his way by two o'clock the next morning.

The Battle of Denmark Strait

As soon as he received the *Suffolk's* message that the *Bismarck* and the *Prinz Eugen* were approaching Denmark Strait, Vice Admiral Lancelot Holland in the *Hood* turned his ship and the *Prince of Wales* to intercept Lütjens. In May, nights are short at latitudes as far north as Denmark Strait. It was broad daylight when the two admirals saw each other's forces at 5:35 A.M. on May 24.

At 5:52 the *Hood* opened fire at 25,000 yards. Two minutes later the *Bismarck* replied. In a few moments hits were scored on each side, and a fire broke out on the *Hood*. Still the two British ships pressed toward the Germans. Suddenly, at exactly 6:00 A.M., another

59

15-inch shell hit the *Hood,* penetrating to her powder magazine. The great ship blew up, broke into two parts, and sank almost immediately. Out of more than 1,500 men on board, only three were saved by escorting destroyers.

The *Prince of Wales,* veering sharply to avoid the *Hood's* smoking wreckage, continued the fight, and scored one or two more hits on the *Bismarck.* But her turret machinery was not working well, and her guns were firing slowly. The *Bismarck,* however, continued to fire rapidly and with remarkable accuracy, and soon inflicted heavy damage on the *Prince of Wales.* After the British battleship's bridge had been wrecked, and four of her ten big guns had been knocked out of action, Captain Leach turned her away from the fight. In company with the *Suffolk* and the *Norfolk,* he followed the two German ships as they steamed south from Denmark Strait into the North Atlantic.

Two of the shells from the *Prince of Wales* had damaged the *Bismarck.* They had hit below the waterline, and one had penetrated a fuel tank. But even though her speed was slightly reduced, and she was trailing oil behind, Admiral Lütjens had decided to continue with the mission, rather than turn back to Germany.

The Chase

Admiral Tovey, now about 300 miles to the east with his three big ships, raced ahead to intercept the two German vessels. At the same time the Admiralty sent out word to the battleships *Rodney,* *Ramillies,* and *Revenge* to leave their convoys and head for the central North Atlantic to help track down the raiders. Admiral Somerville's Force H was already racing north from Gibraltar, trying to reach the troop convoy before the Germans could arrive.

Farther south and west, Captain Martin, in the cruiser HMS *Dor-*

setshire, decided that his convoy was in no immediate danger. Leaving it under the protection of an armed merchant cruiser, he steamed north to get into the battle even though he had received no orders.

All through the day of May 24, the *Bismarck* and the *Prinz Eugen* raced south and east, followed by the *Suffolk,* the *Norfolk,* and the *Prince of Wales.* Attack planes from the carrier *Victorious* made several strikes at the *Bismarck,* and got at least two hits with bombs and torpedoes, but these seemed to do no damage to the heavily armored German ship. At dusk the *Bismarck* turned on her followers and exchanged a few shots with them. Then she resumed her former course, still followed by the British ships. Lütjens had made this maneuver, apparently, to let the *Prinz Eugen* slip away. That ship was low on fuel, and the German admiral wanted her to meet a German tanker that was waiting far to the south, off the ship lanes. The *Prinz Eugen* got away, refueled at sea, and reached Brest about ten days later.

During the night, by a clever maneuver, Lütjens broke contact with the *Suffolk* despite that ship's radar. As the three British ships searched anxiously, the *Bismarck* evidently made a complete turn around them, then resumed her former course to the south and east. Lütjens had decided to head for Brest. He sent a long radio report back to Germany, which was picked up by British radio direction finders.

The Search

As SOON as the reports of the directional signals were received on the *King George V,* Admiral Tovey had them plotted on a map. Unfortunately they were plotted incorrectly, and Tovey, convinced that Lütjens was trying to return to the North Sea between Iceland and

Scotland, ordered his ships to change course to intercept the supposed course of the *Bismarck*. But instead of heading northeast, the German battleship was still going southeast, at better than 25 knots.

A few hours later the Admiralty replotted the directional signals and informed Tovey that the *Bismarck* seemed to be heading for Brest. After another recheck, Tovey ordered all of his ships to change course. Somehow or other the order was not received on HMS *Rodney*, whose nine 16-inch guns would have enabled her to fight on almost even terms with the faster, more heavily armored *Bismarck*. The afternoon of May 26 the *Rodney* crossed in front of the German vessel, and continued on ahead. Neither battleship saw the other. A few hours later the *Rodney* changed course to the southeast, but by this time the *Bismarck* was ahead of her.

The chase continued during the night and into the next morning. By this time many of the British ships were running low on fuel. With the *Bismarck* still undiscovered, there was gloom throughout the fleet and in the Admiralty. Then, late in the morning, a long-range patrol plane from England caught sight of the *Bismarck*. A few minutes later she was also sighted by scouting planes from the *Ark Royal*.

This was good news and bad news. At least the British now knew where the German battleship was. But she was only 700 miles west of Brest. Unless she could be stopped or slowed down before dark, she would be protected by German planes based in France, and would reach port some time the next day. The only vessels that were close enough to intercept her were those of Somerville's Force H. The *Renown*, a battle cruiser older and weaker than the *Hood*, would have no chance against the *Bismarck*. The only hope was that planes from the *Ark Royal* could slow the *Bismarck* down enough so that the *Rodney* and the *King George V* could catch up. The other four battleships and the *Victorious* had returned to their convoys, or

62

steamed to the nearest port to get fuel.

The weather was stormy and overcast. Each time the *Ark Royal* slammed into a great ocean wave her flight deck heaved into the air some sixty feet, then rolled slowly back down. Nevertheless, her torpedo planes took off and searched northward for the *Bismarck*.

The cruiser *Sheffield*, meanwhile, had dashed ahead to get in contact with the German ship. By chance, as the *Ark Royal's* planes flew through the murky sky, they caught sight of the *Sheffield* before they saw the *Bismarck*. Not knowing any other ship was nearby, and not seeing well through the overcast, they dived down to drop their torpedoes on the British cruiser. By rapid and skillful evasive maneuvers the *Sheffield* avoided the torpedoes and, understanding what had happened, did not fire back at the planes. This made the last pilot realize that they had made a mistake. As he flew back to the *Ark Royal,* he sent a message to the *Sheffield*: "Sorry for the kipper."

Landing successfully on the wildly plunging flight deck of the *Ark Royal,* the planes reloaded and took off again. By this time they knew that the *Sheffield* was in sight of the *Bismarck*. Arriving over the British cruiser again, just before dark, they were directed on to their target. Despite the storm, and despite the evasive maneuvers of the German battleship, at least two of the torpedoes found their mark. One of these, near the stern of the great ship, jammed her rudders and damaged her propellers. The *Bismarck* went briefly out of control. Then, her speed reduced to eight knots, she tried to continue her escape. But, unable to steer properly, she was forced to head into the waves, and thus was turned northwest, the very direction from which the *King George V* and *Rodney* were approaching.

During the night a flotilla of five destroyers, under Captain Vian, tried to get close enough to attack the *Bismarck* with torpedoes. But though the steering mechanism of the great ship was ruined, there was nothing wrong with her fire-direction radar or her gunnery. The British vessels were forced to turn away. Apparently one or two of their torpedoes hit the German ship, but they caused no important damage.

Early on the morning of May 28 the *Rodney* and the *King George V* came up within range of their wounded quarry. Soon after they opened fire, the *Bismarck* replied. But the German gunnery was not so good as it had been. The crews were exhausted after four sleepless days and nights. Just as the *Bismarck* was getting the range to the *Rodney*, the British shells began to hit home. Soon the *Bismarck's* fire-direction system was knocked out, and though her guns continued to fire individually, they were very inaccurate. Within an hour and a half all of the guns on the *Bismarck* had been silenced by a hail of heavy shells. She lay heaving on the waves, stopped, and burning fiercely.

The British battleships closed in, trying to sink the defenseless but still defiant ship. But the great 15-inch and 16-inch shells seemed to have little effect against the marvelous protection of the battered warship's hull. Finally, his big ships low on ammunition and almost out of fuel, Admiral Tovey had to order the fight to stop. The honor of sinking the *Bismarck* would have to go to the only other nearby ship that still had torpedoes. This was the *Dorsetshire,* which had just arrived, and was not even supposed to be near the battle. She fired two torpedoes into the blazing hulk. The *Bismarck* turned over and sank. Then, with one of Vian's destroyers, the *Dorsetshire* began to pick up survivors. But after rescuing 110, the arrival of a U-boat forced them to move away. The submarine rescued five more men; nearly 2,300 had gone down with the *Bismarck*.

Later, in the British Admiralty, some officials urged that Captain Martin of the *Dorsetshire* should be court-martialed for having left

64

his convoy without orders. Admiral Sir Dudley Pound, First Sea Lord of the Admiralty, chuckled and said, "I think we can afford to be lenient." He pinned a medal on Captain Martin.

The sinking of the *Bismarck* was a turning point in the war at sea. It did not mean that the British were winning, but it was the end of an important period of the war. Having failed in this dramatic and gallant effort to challenge Britain's mastery of the ocean's surface, the Germans would never again send one of their big ships out into the North Atlantic. Henceforward they would rely upon the U-boat as their only important weapon in the still-desperate Battle of the Atlantic.

Index

Achilles, 20, 22, 23
Admiral Scheer, 53-55
Ajax, 20, 22, 46
Algiers, 38
Altmark, 18, 26, 27
Ark Royal, 40, 59, 62, 63
Athenia (British liner), 1-3 .

Bartolomeo Colleoni, 46
Bismarck, 55-64

Chamberlain, Neville, 3
Churchill, Winston, 3, 4, 13, 34, 43
City of Flint, 16
Cossack (Russian destroyer), 27
Courageous, 10
Crete, 49, 51, 52
Cumberland, 24
Cunningham, Andrew, 38, 45, 46, 49-52

De Gaulle, Charles, 38, 44
Denmark, 29
Denmark Strait, 58, 59
Deutschland, 8, 15, 16
Dorsetshire, 60, 61, 64
Dunkirk, 34-36

Egypt, 48, 49
Exeter, 20, 22

Falkland Islands, 20, 23, 24
Fegen, E. F. S., 53
Force H, 59, 60, 62

Gibraltar, 48
Glorious, 33
Glowworm, 30
Gneisenau, 16, 31, 33, 34, 55
Goering, Hermann, 41
Graf Spee, 8, 15-24
Greece, 49, 51, 52

Harwood, Henry, 20, 22, 23, 24
Hermes, 40
Hipper, 30, 55

Hitler, Adolf, 1
Holland, Lancelot, 59
Hood, 40, 57-60, 62

Iachino, Angelo, 49, 50
Illustrious, 46, 48
Italy, 5, 37, 44

Jean Bart, 38
Jervis Bay, 53
Jossing Fjord, 27

King George V, 57, 58, 61-64
Krancke, Theodore, 53

Langsdorf, Hans, 16-18, 20-24
La Spezia, 51
Lütjens, Günther, 55, 57-61
Lutzow, 31

Malta, 44-46, 48
Matapan, Cape, 49-51
Mediterranean Sea, 5, 6, 37, 38, 44-53
Montevideo, 23, 24
Mussolini, Benito, 5

Narvik, 27, 31-33
Norfolk, 58, 60, 61
North Sea, 7
Norway, 26-33

Operation Sea Lion, 40, 43
Oran, Algeria, 37, 38
Orkney Islands, 10

Pola, 50
Pound, Dudley, 65
Prien, Gunther, 12
Prince of Wales, 57-61
Prinz Eugen, 57, 59, 61

Raeder, Erich, 8
Ramillies, 60
Rawalpindi, 16
Red Sea, 48

66

Renown, 31, 59, 62
Repulse, 58
Resolution, 40
Revenge, 60
Richelieu, 38, 40
Rodney, 60, 62-64
Roosevelt, Franklin D., 43
Royal Oak, 12

Scapa Flow, 10, 57
Scandinavian Straits, 7
Scharnhorst, 16, 33, 34, 55
Sheffield, 59, 63
Sicily, 44, 45
Somerville, James, 38, 39, 48, 49, 58-60
Stavanger, 31
Suffolk, 58-61
Sweden, 7, 27, 29
Sydney, 46

Taranto, 46-48
Tobruk, 46
Toulon, 38, 40
Tovey, John, 57, 60, 61, 64
Trondheim, 31, 33

U-29, 10
U-30, 1
U-47, 12
Uruguay, 23, 24

Valiant, 40
Vian, Philip, 26, 27, 63, 64
Victorious, 58, 61, 62
Vittorio Veneto, 49, 50

Warspite, 33

Yugoslavia, 51